Start Playing Chess

Meet the Characters

Zort from Zugzwang
A teenaged computer from planet Zugzwang, his favorite hobbies are chess, facebook and googling. The star of *Power Chess for Kids*, Zort uses his amazing chess-board vision to teach you how to win!

The chess professor answers kids' questions with wit and wisdom, giving you important winning tips!

Knelly the Knight teaches the special powers of each chess piece. She first appeared in *Power Chess for Kids*, Volume 2.

Power Chess Kids
Chess kids of the world ask typical kids' questions about tricky chess rules and strategy.

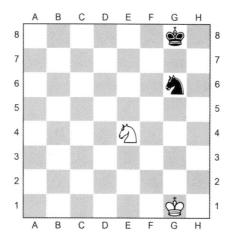

For instance, in this position the move ♘c5 means your knight moves to the c5-square. To find c5, first find the c-file, then the 5th rank, by following the letters and numbers on the edge of the board. Where these lines meet is the c5-square.

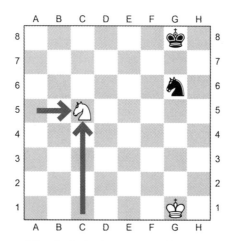

The knight just moved to c5

 That's it?

Basically, yes! Only one more trick and you're ready to begin — *if no piece name is mentioned, only a square, that means a pawn moved to that square.* So in the starting position, if you see the move 1.e4,

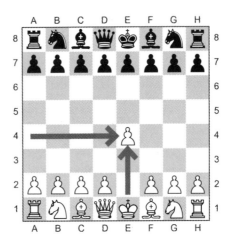

that means on move one, White moved his pawn to the e4-square.

There are a few more add-ons to chess notation we'll mention later, but you already know everything you need to get started!

 OK, I must admit — that *was* easy.

Alright, now let's meet all the pieces, and learn how they move!

The Knight

 The knight is a tricky piece, loved by kids everywhere! Knights move in an 'L' pattern, either two squares forward and one to the side, or one square forward and two to the side. He can also move *backward*, in the same way.

12

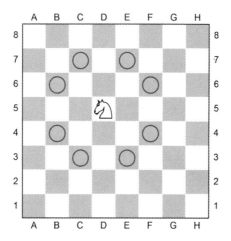

The knight in the diagram can move to any of the 8 squares shown!

Good job, Zort, but don't forget my **super power**! The knight is the only chess piece that can **jump over** its own pieces, or enemy men!

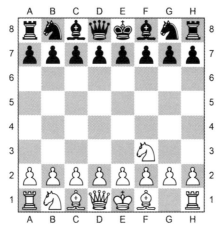

Position after 1.♘f3!

Here White's knight hopped right over its pawns, and moved to f3 to open the game!

The Bishop

The bishop's a unique, cool piece! It moves only **diagonally**, but its **long-range powers** let it move clear across the board, if nothing's in the way.

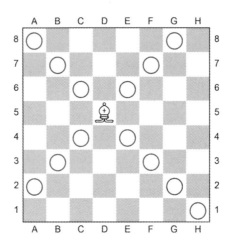

As you can see, a well-placed bishop has many possibilities. It can go diagonally forward to either end of the board, or backward to 'home' territory. The one thing this bishop **can't** do is move on black squares! This 'light-squared' bishop has to stay on the white diagonals. Luckily, each side has two bishops to start the game: one on light squares, one on dark. Between them, the two bishops can attack any square.

The Rook

Some earth kids say they like the bishop or knight better than the rook, but computers prefer the super-mobile rook any day!

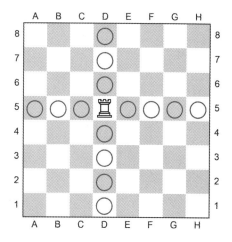

The powerful rook can move any number of squares vertically (forward or backward) or *horizontally* (sideways). Count its huge choice of possible moves if nothing's in the way! Like the bishop, it can sail from one end of the board to another in a single move. But unlike the ♗, it can move on dark or light squares!

This awesome power gives it even more options than the bishop.

The Queen

Any kid will tell you, the queen is super-radical! She's my favorite.

Good choice! The queen is by far the most powerful chess piece. She possesses all the powers of both the *mighty rook*, and the *slippery bishop*.

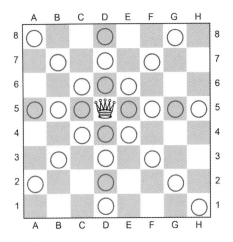

The queen is the **champion** of mobility (options for moving). The unobstructed queen above has an incredible **27** possible moves! She's a 'lean, mean attacking machine' for capturing enemy pieces, or checkmating the king! She moves *vertically* or *horizontally* (like the rook), or *diagonally* (like the bishop), any number of squares, forward or back.

The King

The king is like the 'buried treasure' of the chess board! You better keep him protected, because if you lose him, you lose the game!

Knelly has a good point. The object of a chess game is to **checkmate the enemy king**. We study checkmate thoroughly in Chapter 3, but in a nutshell, it means that the king is under threat of capture, and has no way out.

The king's move is easiest to remember: **one square in any direction**.

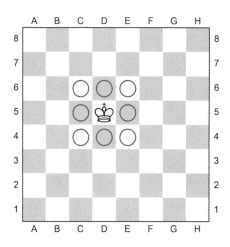

The Pawn

Pawns have the *least* mobility of any piece, but they make up for it in *numbers*, and with an **incredible** super-power!

That's right! Each side has **eight** pawns to start the game, far more than any other piece. The **normal** pawn move is simple: one square straight ahead.

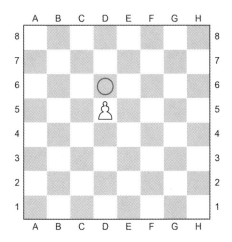

True, but...pawns have several **exceptional** moves they make in certain situations, which make learning *all* the pawn moves more difficult than any other piece. For starters, **pawns are the only piece which can't move backward**. They're also the only piece with an **extra option** on their *first move of the game*:

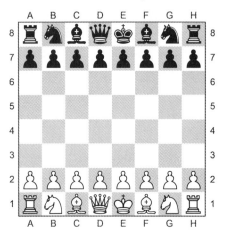

Any pawn can move **one or two squares on its first move of the game**, so for instance the e-pawn can move 1 or 2 squares on move one:

1.e2-e4, the King's Pawn Opening

The e-pawn started with a 2-square move, but from now on it goes just one square. Any other pawn can move one or two squares for its first move, but only one after that.

I would suggest *moving the pawns in front of your king and queen two squares* on their first move, as long as they can't be captured right away. These pawns in the middle or *center* have more attacking power if you move them two squares, and also leave your other pieces *more space* to move around.

What about the **super-power** you mentioned earlier?

Knelly was talking about **pawn promotion**. This crazy pawn move is so important that we give it a special section in Chapter 4, along with cool **castling**, and the *weirdest* pawn move, the en passant capture.

The pawn has one more unique feature: it's the only chess piece that **captures differently than it normally moves**! We cover that next, along with all you need to know about *captures*.

Chapter 2: Captures – Take That!

Every chess piece has the power to **capture** ('take') enemy chessmen! Learning how to capture enemy pieces is pretty easy, once you master how the pieces move. The hard part is being alert enough to notice when you can take an enemy piece, and noticing when your own pieces can be taken.

All chess pieces capture the same way they normally move, except the pawn.

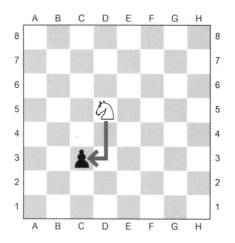

You learned that knights move in L-shapes, as shown above. Here Black's pawn is sitting on a square that White's knight *attacks*. To capture the pawn, White's knight moves two squares back, one to the left, **landing on the c3-square occupied by the pawn, and removing Black's pawn from the board**.

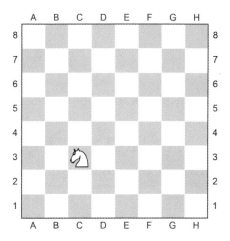

White's knight captured the black pawn on c3

Remember the great first move 1.e4 ? One of Black's worst answers is 1...b5? (the question mark means 'bad move').

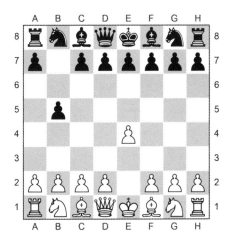

 That's a stinky move!

Very alert! This silly move is called a 'blunder' – a move that simply loses a chessman for nothing. White snaps up the pawn with his long-range bishop:

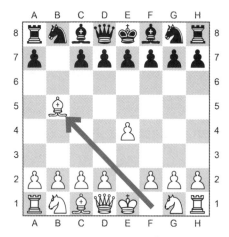

Position after 2.♗xb5

*(the 'x' in chess notation means 'captures'
– bishop captures the pawn on b5)*

No black piece can *recapture* White's bishop, so White just won a free pawn!

Here's a little quiz to make sure you understand how captures work. What if White didn't see the capture and moved ♘f3, and Black answered with ♘a6, reaching this position:

White's move — what can he capture?

Wait, I see that White's bishop can still take the pawn, but can he also capture Black's knight behind it?

No, I fooled you! He can't take the knight because he'd have to *jump over* the enemy pawn, and only knights can jump over other pieces. The best move for White is still to capture the pawn on b5 (3.♗xb5). Then let's say Black moves the other ♘ to f6.

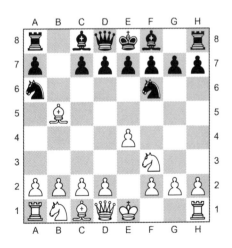

Interesting! Next move Black's knight could *capture* the e-pawn.

Right! A move that gives the possibility of taking an enemy man next move is called a **threat**. To *escape* the threat in the position below there are two options. The first is to *move the piece* out of attack – White advances his pawn one square to e5.

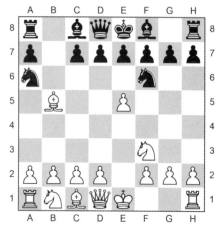

White's pawn moved away, and is no longer *under attack* from Black's knight

The second option is called *protecting* the attacked piece. Instead of advancing the pawn, White could **protect** it by moving ♘c3:

You can always use these values to figure out who comes out ahead when both sides make a capture. So in the previous position, Black made a *stinkbomb* blunder! He lost two points, getting only a pawn for a knight.

Let's see some **capture action** by other pieces:

White's powerful queen has three possible captures. Can you find them?

Answer: The queen could take three different pawns, on a7, d7, or g7. Taking the pawn on a7 is great, and will even get Black's rook on b8 next move! Taking on g7 is bad, because the black bishop on f8 *protects* the pawn, and can recapture White's queen! Taking the d7-pawn is also terrible – Black *recaptures* (takes back) with either his bishop, queen or king and says 'ha – I got your queen for just a pawn!'

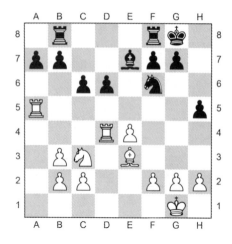

White's two combined rooks can capture three different pawns between them, but only one is a good deal. The pawn on a7 is *unprotected*, so 1.♖xa7! is great (an exclamation point means a good move). The other two rook captures on d6 or h5 are **blunders**, allowing Black to recapture with his bishop or knight.

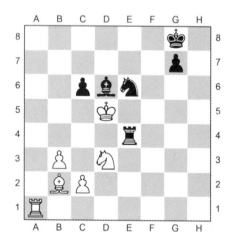

This position is called an **endgame** because most pieces were traded off. The white king was finally safe enough to come out and attack! Which black pieces can he capture here? Which would you take?

Answer: White can take the rook, bishop, or pawn, but not the knight, which is *protected* by Black's rook (in the next chapter you will learn why the king isn't allowed to move into attack!). Naturally, he should take Black's strongest man, the 5-point valued rook!

Pawn Captures

We save the tricky one for last! As mentioned earlier, *pawns are the only chess piece that capture differently than they normally move.* **Pawns can capture only** diagonally, one square ahead. This weird rule takes getting used to!

If White starts a game with the familiar **1.e4**, Black's *other* worst move is **1...f5?**

White can now *capture* the black pawn one diagonal square ahead:

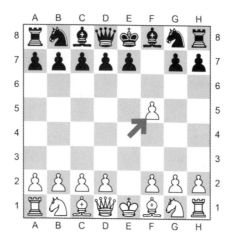

2.e4xf5! Black can't take back, so he lost a pawn!

On the other hand, one of Black's *best* first moves is to copy White with 1...e5.

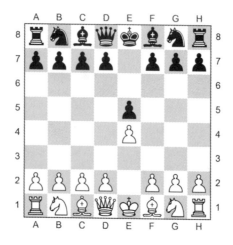

1...e7-e5 The 'double king pawn opening' At first glance this looks like a mistake – but it's not! Know what I *mean*, **jelly bean**?

Yes, of course! White's e-pawn **can't** capture Black's, because pawns only capture one square ahead **diagonally** – not straight ahead! Which black pieces can White's pawns capture in the next diagram?

Watch out for Knelly's sneaky tricks! Only the pawn high-lighted above has two pieces **one square diagonally ahead** of it – and of course he should take the mighty queen! He can't take the knight or bishop anyway, because **pawns never move backwards**.

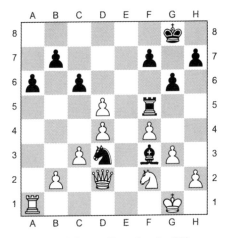

Position after 1.e4xd5!

For extra credit, find the three ways Black can at least recapture the white pawn.

Chapter 3: Check, Checkmate and Stalemate

 OK kids, now you know *almost* everything about how the pieces move and capture. But before you learn the rest, we have to cover something equally important: attacking the enemy KING! Remember this very important fact:

The object of a chess game is to checkmate the enemy king, not to capture all his pieces!

Capturing pieces is very important to improve your *chances* of checkmating, but there is no substitute for knowing how to finish him off by delivering mate ('Mate' is a chessplayer's nickname for 'checkmate').

Check

A check in chess is a move that threatens to capture the enemy king next move.

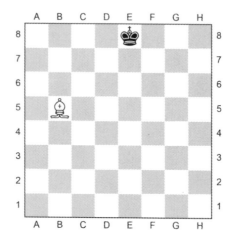

In the diagram above, White's bishop has put the black king in **check** – his bishop makes a **direct attack** on the enemy king. (*Direct attack* means a threat to take an enemy piece next move).

The Three Ways to Get Out of Check

When your opponent puts you in check, don't panic! Not all checks are good moves; in fact, some are even blunders. The important thing is to *always consider the three ways to escape check*, then figure out which one to use:

Option 1: Capture the checking piece

This is often the best option when it's possible! In the diagram below, White has blundered by taking a *protected* pawn with his queen.

White's queen gives **check**, a direct threat to take Black's king, but...

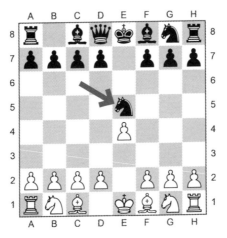

1...♘xe5! – Goodbye queen!
Black's knight makes it's L shaped **capture** – two squares over and one up – and wins the reckless white queen for only a pawn!

Option 2 for escaping check: Interposing

The fancy chess term *interposing* means putting your piece **in between** your king and the checking piece, to shield your king from capture. Here's a position where White gives check on the second move(!); but Black defends strongly by interposing:

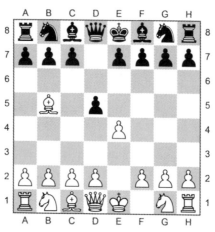

White just played 2.♗b5+
(the plus sign means 'check'!)

White's bishop advanced to check Black's king, and the king has nowhere to run! Luckily, *he doesn't have to:* he can **interpose** strongly by moving his c-pawn:

2...c7-c6, *stopping* **the check**

Black's pawn comes **in between** the enemy bishop and his king, shielding him from check. Better yet – remember how pawns capture *one square ahead diagonally?* The black pawn now threatens to capture White's bishop, so White must waste time by moving the bishop backward. If White captures 3.♗xc6+?, Black takes back with his b-pawn or knight, winning a bishop for a pawn.

Option 3 for escaping check: Move the King

Here the white rook made a long-distance check on Black's king. Black's rook could move all the way back to d8 and interpose, but this is bad here; White's rook would capture Black's for free! Instead Black should **move the king** one square up:

1...♔g7, escaping check

Now the king is safe and sound, and White's check didn't accomplish much.

Can you guess why I saved **moving the king** for last, even though it's the easiest way to escape check? Because kids usually grab their kings right away when they're in check, and forget to consider the other options!

Computers do the opposite! If taking the checking piece or interposing are possible, they're usually **better** than moving the king, especially early in the game!

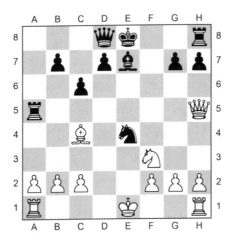

White just played **1.♕h5+**.

Here Black has *all three options* to escape the check by White's queen. He could **interpose** by moving his g-pawn up one to block the check:

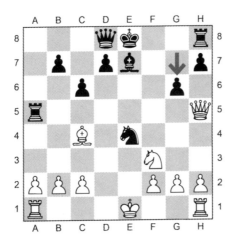

This move effectively blocks the check, but isn't best by a long shot! Better is Option 1, capturing the checking queen with his distant rook!

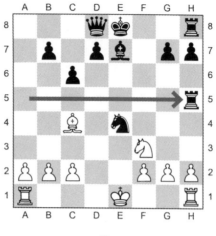

1...♖xh5!

Proves the check was a blunder! White's queen check was a big-league boo-boo – only because Black was very alert, and looked at every possibility to **capture** the checking piece. But what if Black was lazy and just played option 3, **moving the king**? That brings us to the next topic:

Checkmate!

Position after 1...♔f8??, moving the king to escape the check – yuchh!

By taking the queen Black would have great winning chances, but *moving the king* instead loses at once – White's queen swoops in to f7 for **checkmate**!

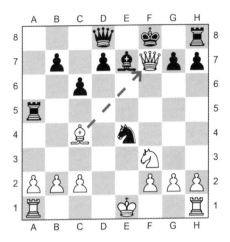

2.♕f7# – Checkmate! (*the tic-tac-toe board means 'checkmate'*).

A **checkmate** is a special kind of check – the *best* kind! You can see above that Black's king is in check – White's queen *directly* *threatens* to take him next move. Checkmate **means that none of the 3 options for escaping check works**. Black's king *can't* *move away* to safety – if he moves to the side, the queen still gets him with her diagonal powers. He can't *interpose* either – the white queen is so close, there's no room to put a piece between her and Black's king. But what about the last option, *capturing the checking piece*? If you look carefully, only Black's king is in position to do that, but he can't because **White's bishop on c4 would get him** (it *protects* the queen).

Moving your king into check is called an **illegal move** in chess – it's not allowed. Taking White's queen with the king is an *illegal* move due to the bishop's *protection*, so Black has no possible way to escape the check – it's **checkmate!** *Checkmate means the game is over* – *White wins!*

A knight's tip about **illegal moves** – sorry kids, but if you put your opponent in check and he doesn't see it, you're *not allowed* to take his king! By staying in check he made an *illegal move* – and unfortunately you have to let him take it back! If he has any way to escape the check by taking your piece, interposing, or moving the king, he **has** to do it – but if he *can't*, congratulations! You win by checkmate.

King and Queen Checkmate

One of the most important, but easiest checkmates to learn, is the *mate* with king and queen against a lone king. It's so important because if you win the enemy queen, you can usually trade the other pieces and checkmate him with your ♔+♕ working together:

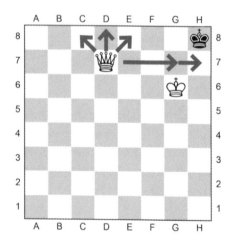

If you can chase the opposing king to the edge of the board, or even better, the *corner*, delivering checkmate is *much* easier. See for yourself: in the middle of the board a king has 8 possible moves, but when cornered like Black's king above, he has only 3 possible escape squares! Here White is set up perfectly for two different kinds of checkmate – the **back rank mate**, and the **queen protected by king** mate. To deliver the back rank mate, White moves his queen forward to c8, d8, or e8:

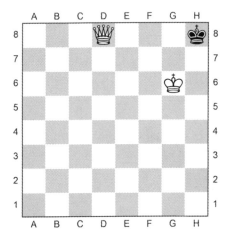

1.♕d8# – Back Rank Checkmate

It's called a 'back rank' mate because the queen *checks* on the back (eighth) rank, and covers all back rank *escape squares*. Meanwhile, White's king guards the two *forward* escape squares – the black king can't come up, because White's will **take** him, which makes advancing the black king an **illegal move**. (Remember? The king is not allowed to move into capture – so moving your king one square away from his king is *always* illegal.) Black's king is in check, but he has no other pieces to capture the queen or interpose, and no safe *escape* squares to move out of check.

 CHECKMATE!!

 Right-O, you're getting the hang of it.
In the previous diagram, White could also checkmate by sliding his ♕ over to g7 (or h7):

41

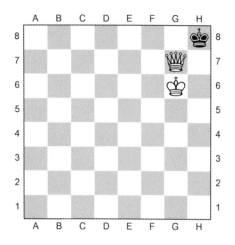

1.♕g7# – The ♕ protected by ♔ mate

It's easy to see that White's ♕ checks the black king and covers his escape squares, but this time the queen can't be captured because the white king *protects* her – **checkmate**!

Both these crucial mates show the importance of *teamwork* in chess: rarely can a piece deliver checkmate by itself – even the mighty queen needs support, in this case by the white king!

Stalemate

 Ugh, stalemate is a kid's worst nightmare!

 Yeah, kids always google how to avoid stalemate when they're way ahead.

A **stalemate** is very *similar* to checkmate, with two **extremely important** differences! In the position we just looked at, the **worst move** for White would be moving his queen very close to the enemy king, but **without** a check: 1.♕f7??

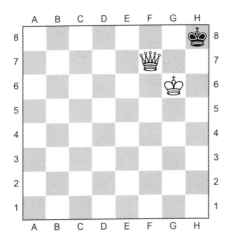

Position after 1.♕f7?? Draw by Stalemate!!

Instead of checkmating on the back rank, or protected by the king, White moved his queen very *close* the enemy king. It looks good, because Black can't legally move his king, take or interpose – but there's one huge problem! The black king *isn't in check!!* White's queen failed to make a **direct threat** to capture the king next move.

If the enemy king is in check and he has no legal escape moves, it's checkmate – you win. **But if the enemy king is** not in check **and he has no legal moves, it's stalemate** – and the game is a **draw**, which means a tie! A draw is still better than a loss – in tournament play, a win is worth 1 point, a draw is a ½ point, and a loss is no points. But a win is much better than a draw! What a shame for White to allow stalemate, when he had instant checkmate!

If Black had one extra piece left in the last diagram, it could actually help White!

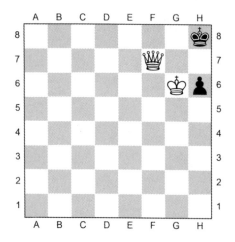

With the extra pawn, Black isn't *in stalemate* because he has a legal move – he **can and must** move the pawn (**1...h5**); then White delivers either type of checkmate we learned. One strategy to avoid stalemate is to leave the opponent one piece like that pawn, which isn't bothering White anyway – but an even better strategy is just to be super alert: if you move your queen very close to the enemy king **without giving check**, *make sure he has at least one legal move!*

Chapter 4: The Trickiest Chess Moves

Castling, Pawn Promotion, and En Passant Pawn Capture

Castling

Castling is the only chess move that lets two of your pieces move on the same turn! This makes it a unique and important option. Castling involves your king and a rook. The basic move isn't too hard to learn – **king goes over two squares, and rook hops over the king and lands on the square next to it**.

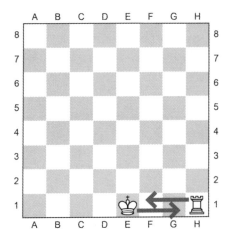

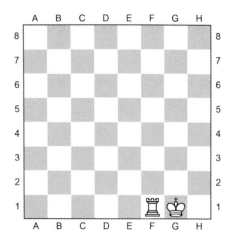

White has completed castling

When White castles with his *other* rook he still uses the same formula – king over two squares, rook hops over. But the end position looks a little different because there is more space between the king and the rook on the *queen's side* of the board.

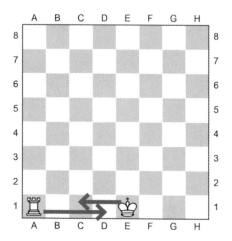

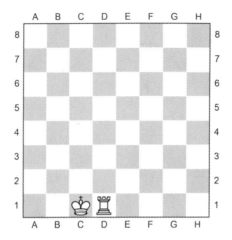

White has castled queenside

These diagrams show the *first special rule about castling* – **To castle, there must be no pieces in between your king and rook.**

OK, castling is cool, but what's so great about it?

Sharp question. Remember we saw earlier that pieces have more mobility (good options) in the center of the board? Because of this, a lot of action happens in the center. So the center is a good area for your rook to be, but a bad place to keep your king!

The king needs to carefully avoid getting checkmated! So instead of being near the action, he wants to be tucked safely in a corner, with pawns protecting him. Castling is a fantastic move, because it helps your king **and** rook. The king finds a safe shelter, and the rook gets more attacking chances, all in one move! This is why some of the best chess openings (moves at the beginning of the game) involve early castling, sometimes on the fourth move!

This is the famous **Ruy Lopez Opening**. White has made three perfect moves! First, pawn to e4, attacking the center and opening lines for the bishop and queen. Next, ♘ to f3, getting the knight out to his best attacking square; and finally, bishop to b5, an active but safe square for the bishop, which pressures Black's knight on c6. Now there are no men between his king and ♖ on h1, so White can already **castle** strongly – 4.0-0!

Position after 4.0-0! (0-0 *is the special chess notation for castling on the 'short' side [king's side]. Castling on the queen's side is written '0-0-0'*)

This awesome move gives White's king a safe haven, while his rook is ready for central action. In my opening book, *Basic Chess Openings for Kids*, you can even study a great game in the Ruy Lopez Opening, in which White's king castled to safety, and his active rook in the middle was able to attack and **checkmate** Black's king, who forgot to castle and got stuck in the middle of the action!

Castling isn't really *that* tricky, is it?

Yes, I'm afraid it is, and now we have to cover the trickier parts. There are many more **special rules** or 'conditions' about when castling is allowed, and when it isn't. These take some time and practice for kids to learn correctly. Keep the book nearby when you play a game, and you can check this list to make sure you can castle:

1. You can't castle if your king has already moved. This also means each side can only castle once per game. For this reason, try to avoid moving your king in the opening, until you're ready to castle! It's good to keep your *castling privilege*.

2. If your rook has moved, you can't castle with *that* rook. You can still castle with the *other* rook, if neither it nor the king has moved yet.

3. You can't castle *while your king is in check*. However, if you stop the check without moving your king (block the check or take the checking piece), you can still castle later. You *can* castle if only your rook is attacked.

4. Finally, the trickiest condition: your king can't pass *through* a check while castling. In other words, your king can't cross over a square that is *guarded* by an enemy piece:

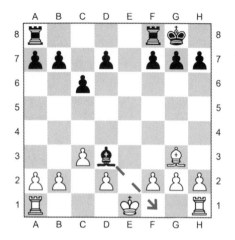

In this position White can't castle to the right ('kingside'), because his king would have to pass through the f1-square, which is guarded by Black's bishop. He **can** castle left ('queenside'), because only the rook would cross through the bishop's attack, and that is allowed.

Castling is such an awesome move, you should practice it every chance you get. Masters castle in over 80% of their games, and mastering castling makes you a **much** better player.

Pawn Promotion

This is definitely one of the weirdest and strongest chess moves, and an all-time kids' favorite! Your humble pawn can be transformed into a *superhero* of the chess board! All you have to do is move him all the way to the back rank. But it's harder than it sounds.

When a pawn reaches the back rank, he gets **promoted** into a stronger piece!! You can, and must, replace him with either a queen, rook, knight or bishop.

White is behind by four points here, but he's about to change all that! He moves his pawn up to the back rank, and promotes it into a new queen. In chess notation, the move is written as 1.e7-e8♕:

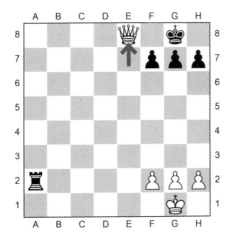

White's pawn **promoted** – with checkmate! When you *promote* a pawn, **the pawn leaves the board and is replaced by the new piece you choose** (*any piece except a pawn or king*). You might have noticed something else special here – Black's king is in **checkmate**! White's new queen delivered a *back rank checkmate*, with Black's own pawns blocking the king's escape.

Two questions: can you promote a pawn into a queen if you already have a queen on the board? And why would anyone ever promote to anything except a queen? She's the best piece by far!

Two *excellent* questions, with surprising answers! First, yes. It's possible for one side to have two queens, or even more! In this position between two famous *grandmasters*, Judit Polgar and Alexander Khalifman, both sides *promoted* pawns and had two queens on the board at the same time.

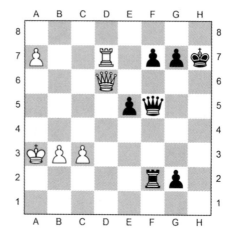

First White promoted her advanced pawn into a queen **1.a8♕**, then Black did the same, **1...g1♕**, reaching the following amazing position:

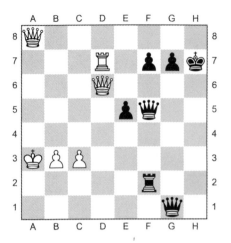

Position after 1...g2-g1♛

Together the four queens have so much firepower, one side can usually checkmate quickly in such rare positions. Black won in four more moves, because his king was safer from enemy checks. By the way, if you don't have a spare queen, kids use an upside-down rook, or a piece turned sideways, to represent the second queen.

As for your **second** question, you should *almost* always promote your pawn into a queen, but there are rare positions in which underpromotion (promoting to a lesser piece) is even stronger! Look at this *very* tricky position:

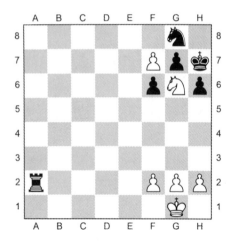

White has many ways to promote his pawn on the back rank, but the *best* way is a gigantic surprise! First, he could *capture* Black's knight and promote his pawn into a queen:

1.f7xg8♕+?

(To explain this funny-looking move: White's f-pawn captures Black's knight on g8, and promotes to a queen, giving *check* – but the question mark shows it was a blunder!)

Position after 1.f7xg8♕+?

What's the problem? Black's king captures the queen with a two point lead – **1...♚xg8**.

So White says 'wait a minute – if I just move my pawn ahead one (instead of taking the knight) and make a queen, his king can't get me!'

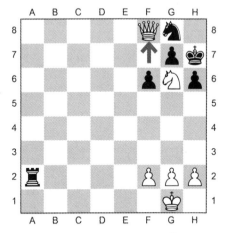

Position after 1.f7-f8♕??

Great idea *except* for one problem – Black's rook then moves forward and delivers **back rank checkmate:1...♖a1#!**
White gained a queen, but lost the game!

Position after 1...♖a1#!

Look carefully – White is checkmated! Black's rook **directly attacks** (checks) White's king on the first rank. The king can't move to h1 or f1 – the rook *controls* these squares, and would get him. But he can't escape forward, either – the king is *blocked* in by his own pawns on f2, g2, and h2. This is the most common version of **back rank mate**.

Instead of giving up, White thinks **really hard** and finds the only **winning** option – the pawn advances one square, but *underpromotes* into a new **knight**!!

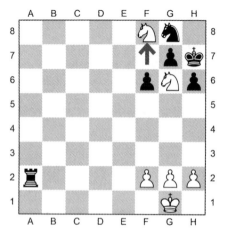

Position after 1.f7-f8♘#!!

CHECKMATE! The new knight checks Black's king, and protects his other knight on g6, who controls the Black king's only escape hatch on h8. Black's rook can't checkmate White now, *because the game is already over!* This beautiful position shows exactly why **checkmating the king is even more important than winning material!** ('Winning material' means taking enemy men, or coming out ahead in points.) White got less *material* by underpromoting to a knight, but he gained something much more important – checkmate!! As we said, though, you should *almost always* promote into a queen, unless you see exactly why you shouldn't. Your new queen can usually help you checkmate later and win the game.

The En Passant Pawn Capture

En Passant is the hardest chess rule for kids to learn. In my classes kids rarely know it perfectly, even if they've been playing for a long time. First I have to teach them **the secret** that makes it easier to remember.

Two unique rules about *en passant* make it the **weirdest** chess move!

1. En Passant is the only chess move in which you capture a piece *not on the square it occupies, but instead on a square that it just passed over!!*

2. It's the only chess capture that you can *only make immediately* (next move) after the enemy pawn passes your pawn!! If you don't take his pawn *en passant* right away, that pawn can't be taken *en passant* for the rest of the game.

Here is how **en passant** works:

First, the **en passant capture** is only possible if *one side has a pawn on the fifth rank,* like White's pawn on e5 above. Second, a pawn on the file (vertical line) next to White's pawn has to **move past** it by advancing two squares: 2...d7-d5.

Position after 2...d7-d5

Black's pawn moved two squares to d5, passing a *normal capture* by White's e5-pawn. Now comes the strangest move: **White's e5-pawn takes Black's d-pawn on d6, as if he only moved one square!!!**

Position after 3.e5xd6, en passant

As with any capture, White's pawn removed Black's from the board; but instead of landing on the d5-square where Black's pawn sat (like all other chess captures), he landed on d6, the square Black's pawn passed by (en passant is French for 'in passing' – White's pawn captured Black's in *passing*)!

So what's **the secret** for remembering en passant? Just remember a basic rule of how the pieces move – **pawns can only capture one diagonal square ahead**! *Even in en passant, your pawn takes his, one diagonal square ahead.* But what if White *doesn't* capture in the diagram, but plays **2.d4** instead.

Is he allowed to do that?

Yes! Just because you *can* capture en passant, doesn't mean you *have* to. So after 2.d4 Black plays 2...♗g7, reaching the following position. Now, can White still take the d6-pawn *en passant*?

Position after 3...♗g7

Don't be ridiculous, Knelly! We read the answer – White can only take the d-pawn *en passant* **immediately after** he passed White's pawn – if you wait a move, it's too late!

You chess kids are getting very smart! But say White plays 4.♘c3, and then Black's **f-pawn** moves two squares, passing the white pawn on e5?

Position after 4...f7-f5

Now can White take the f-pawn en *passant*?

Let's see – Black's f-pawn just moved two squares and *passed* a white pawn on the fifth rank – yes!! I *can* take him en passant, one diagonal square ahead!

Position after 5.e5xf6, en passant!

Congratulations! You have now mastered **all** the important rules. The only things we didn't have space to cover were *perpetual check, three-fold repetition, and the 50-move rule,* but these are rare situations that apply mostly to tournament play. You can google them for further study if you like. More importantly, once you've played enough to remember all the rules and put them in practice, you're ready to order **Power Chess for Kids, Volumes 1 & 2,** learn *master tactics* and become one of the strongest players in your school! You can find them in every major (online) book shop or the New In Chess website, now available in print or Kindle. For updates on Zort and all his friends, visit **Power Chess for Kids** on Facebook.

About the Author

American FIDE Chess Master Charles Hertan has been teaching chess to kids of all ages for more than three decades. He believes that kids' great enthusiasm and capacity for learning should be encouraged in every way possible, using humor, a personable style, and top-notch instruction that respects children's innate ability to appreciate the artistic beauty of chess.

Mr. Hertan authored the adult chess tactics book *Forcing Chess Moves*, winner of the prestigious Chess Café Book of the Year Award for 2008. His highly acclaimed tactics manuals for children, *Power Chess for Kids* Volumes 1&2, introduced a fresh, fun and instructionally sound method for helping kids learn the basics of calculation and thinking ahead. He followed this with *Basic Chess Opening for Kids*, covering the most important strategies for getting a good position at the beginning of the game. Hertan's groundbreaking focus on the *thought processes* underlying chess improvement is highlighted in an article he wrote for *The Chess Instructor 2009*, a compendium for chess teachers, coaches and parents.

His first book was a collection of poetry for adults, *Dream Catcher: Selected Poems by Lynn Kernan* (Bunny & Crocodile Press, 2006).

An award-winning author teaches how to weed out silly moves and just consider a few important ones

If you want to amaze your friends with your chess skills, this is exactly the book you have been looking for. To become one of the best chess players in your school you need to play **Power Moves**, winning tactics that require thinking ahead.

"What a wonderful series. This is really a beautiful and instructive book and a lot of children will certainly be enjoying it and getting better because of it."
Lukas Wedrychowski, DailyChess

"The kids I work with got a kick out of it."
Edward Scimia, About.com-CHESS

"When my youngest son saw the book, he immediately got excited. The drawings and the child-friendly lay-out had a magic impact on him."
Martin Rieger, Rochade Europa Magazine